D1295256

MINNESOTA VIKINGS

BY BRIAN HOWELL

Published by The Child's World®
1980 Lookout Drive • Mankato, MN 56003-1705
800-599-READ • www.childsworld.com

Acknowledgments
The Child's World®: Mary Berendes, Publishing Director
Red Line Editorial: Editorial direction
The Design Lab: Design
Amnet: Production

Design Element: Dean Bertoncelj/Shutterstock Images
Photographs ©: Reinhold Matay/AP Images, cover; NFL Photos/AP Images, 5; Ann Heisenfelt/AP Images, 7; Bettmann/Corbis, 9; Allen Fredrickson/Icon Sportswire, 11; PRNewsFoto/Minnesota Sports Facilities Authority/AP Images, 13; Andy Blenkush/AP Images, 14–15; Marilyn Indahl/Icon Sportswire, 17; AP Images, 19; Stephen Bartholomew/Actionplus/Icon Sportswire, 21; Vince Muzik/Icon Sportswire, 23; Doug Murray/Icon Sportswire, 25; Ric Tapia/Icon Sportswire, 27; Vernon Biever/AP Images, 29

ISBN 9781634070102
LCCN 2014959715

Printed in the United States of America
Mankato, MN
July, 2015
PA02265

ABOUT THE AUTHOR

Brian Howell is a freelance writer based in Denver, Colorado. He has been a sports journalist for nearly 20 years and has written dozens of books about sports and two about American history. A native of Colorado, he lives with his wife and four children in his home state.

TABLE OF CONTENTS

GO, VIKINGS!

The Minnesota Vikings started playing in 1961. They have been one of the best pro football teams since then. They are often in the hunt for the **playoffs**. The Vikings also had one of the greatest sports nicknames of all time. Minnesota had a fearsome defensive line in the 1960s and 1970s. Those players were called "The Purple People Eaters." Let's meet the Vikings.

"The Purple People Eaters" were a tough group that featured Hall of Famers Carl Eller (81) and Alan Page (88).

70
77
81

WHO ARE THE VIKINGS?

The Minnesota Vikings play in the National Football **League** (NFL). They are one of the 32 teams in the NFL. The NFL includes the American Football Conference (AFC) and the National Football Conference (NFC). The winner of the NFC plays the winner of the AFC in the **Super Bowl**. The Vikings play in the North Division of the NFC. The Vikings have played in four Super Bowls. But they are still looking for their first championship.

Randy Moss (84) grew into one of the best wide receivers in the NFL while with the Vikings.

WHERE THEY CAME FROM

The Vikings joined the NFL in 1961. Minnesota was nicknamed the Vikings for two reasons. The first was that Vikings are known as tough and rugged. The second was because of the history of the state. Many Minnesota **citizens** have family ties to a part of the world called Scandinavia. Vikings were tough guys from that area. The team got off to a winning start. Minnesota beat the Chicago Bears 37–13 in its first game on September 17, 1961.

Vikings fullback Bill Brown (right) runs with the ball during Minnesota's first Super Bowl appearance on January 11, 1970.

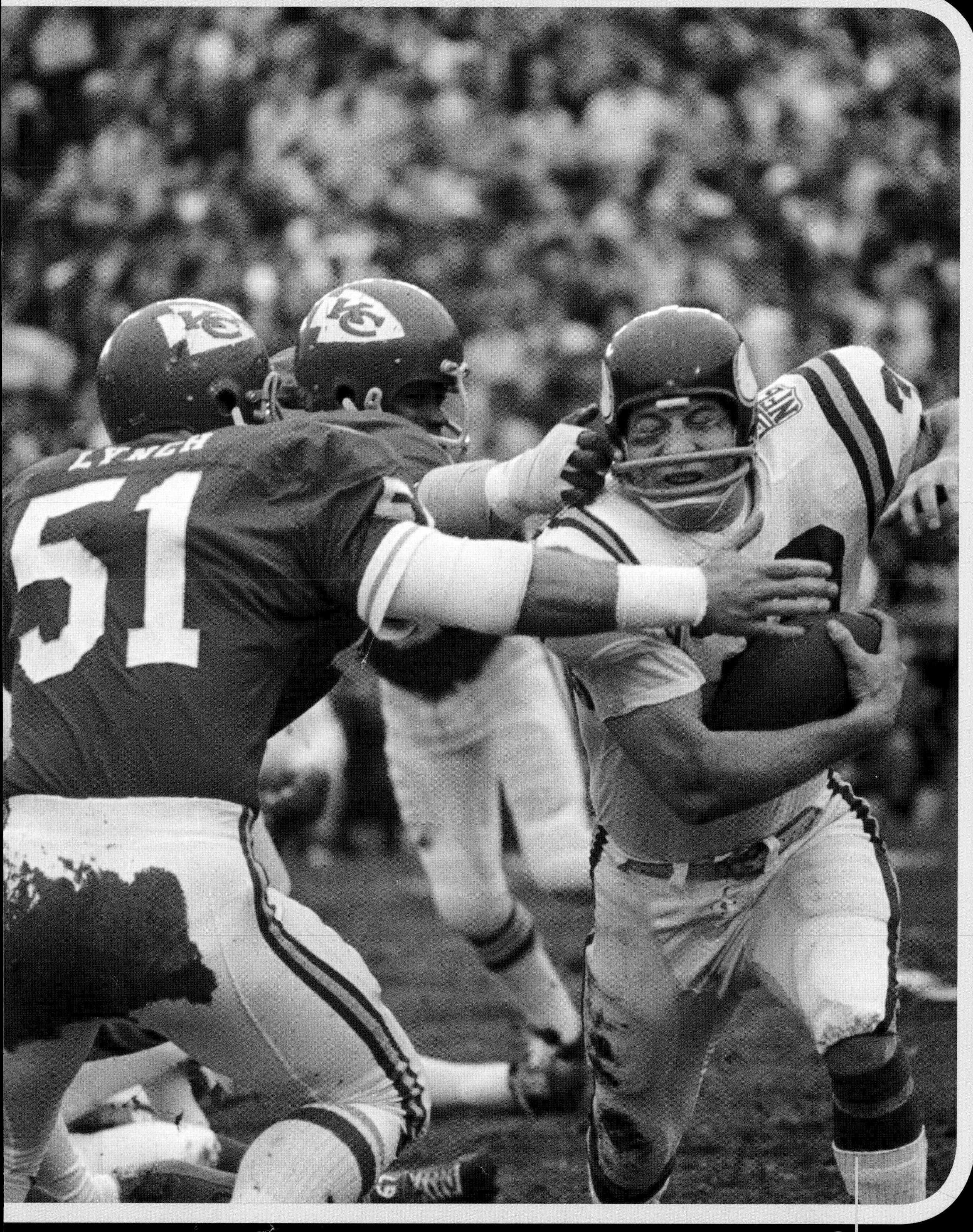
LYNCH
51

WHO THEY PLAY

The Minnesota Vikings play 16 games each season. With so few games, each one is important. Every year, the Vikings play two games against each of the other three teams in their division. Those teams are the Chicago Bears, Detroit Lions, and Green Bay Packers. The Vikings also play six other teams from the NFC and four from the AFC. Green Bay is in Wisconsin. It borders Minnesota. That has made the Vikings and Packers **rivals**.

Games between the Vikings and Packers are often heated because Minnesota and Wisconsin are border states.

25

WHERE THEY PLAY

The Vikings played in Metropolitan Stadium from 1961 to 1981. Then they moved to the Metrodome. But it got old. In 2010, there was a giant snowstorm. It caused part of the stadium's roof to collapse. The Vikings stuck it out in the Metrodome until 2013. But then it was time for a new stadium. Construction on the new stadium began in 2014. TCF Bank Stadium was the Vikings' temporary home during construction. TCF Bank Stadium is the home of the University of Minnesota football team.

Vikings fans were excited about their team's new home, shown in this 2013 drawing.

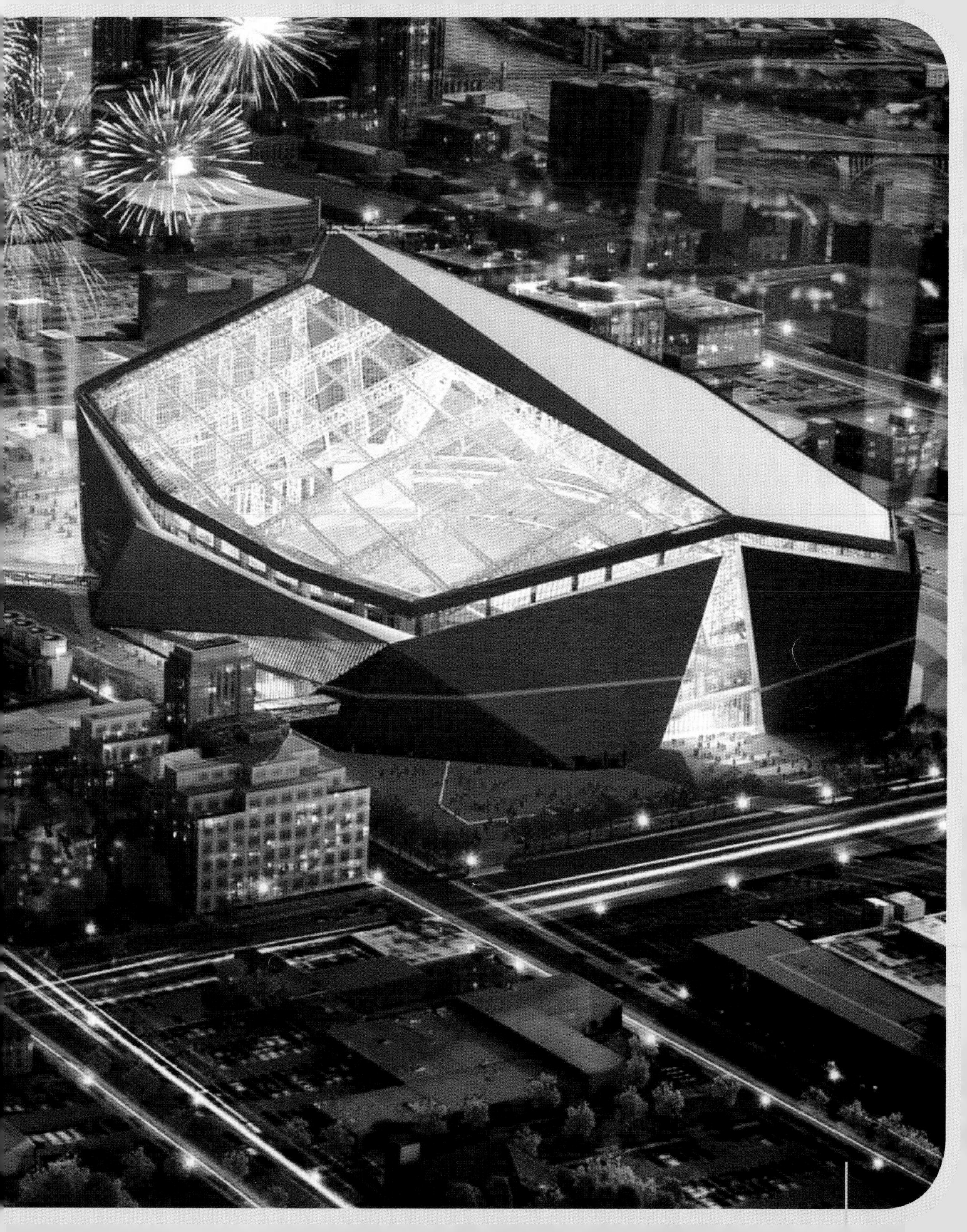

THE FOOTBALL FIELD

GOAL LINE

END LINE

MIDFIELD

BENCH AREA

END ZONE

GOAL POST
20-YARD LINE
SIDELINE
HASH MARKS

BIG DAYS

The Vikings have had some great moments in their history. Here are three of the greatest:

1969—Minnesota had played its first playoff game in 1968. The next year, the Vikings did even better. They went 12-2 during the regular season. Then they won two playoff games. That took Minnesota to its first Super Bowl. It was the first of four Super Bowl trips under coach Bud Grant.

1998—This was perhaps the team's greatest season. The Vikings won a team-record 15 games. They scored 556 points. That was an NFL record. **Rookie** wide receiver Randy Moss became a star. He led the NFL with 17 **touchdown** catches.

Quarterback Brett Favre made the Pro Bowl and led Minnesota to the NFC Championship Game in the first of his two seasons with the Vikings.

2009—Brett Favre was a Green Bay Packers legend. He had many great games against the Vikings. But he joined Minnesota in 2009. It was a great move. The Vikings went 12–4 and reached the NFC Championship Game.

TOUGH DAYS

Football is a hard game. Even the best teams have rough games and seasons. Here are some of the toughest times in Vikings history:

1962—Minnesota's second season was its worst. The Vikings went 2-11-1. They were overmatched in many of their games. They allowed almost 30 points per game. That was the worst in the NFL.

1975—The Vikings made the playoffs. They played the Dallas Cowboys on December 28. Minnesota led 14-10 with 32 seconds left. Cowboys quarterback Roger Staubach threw a long touchdown pass to wide receiver Drew Pearson. Dallas won 17-14. It is known as the first "Hail Mary" play.

Wide receiver Drew Pearson (88) broke the hearts of Vikings fans when his "Hail Mary" catch knocked Minnesota out of the playoffs on December 28, 1975.

2010—The Metrodome was the Vikings' home. But on December 12, the roof collapsed under heavy snow. Luckily, nobody was hurt. Minnesota's final two home games of the season were moved.

MEET THE FANS

Vikings fans have been behind their team from the start. Sports fans in Minnesota are loyal. And the Vikings are the most popular team in town. Fans show up for games even during bad seasons. Many of them wear Viking gear to the stadium. This includes helmets with horns. Minnesota's mascot is named Viktor.

Minnesota fans love dressing up in Viking gear when they come out to support their team.

HEROES THEN

Fran Tarkenton was Minnesota's first quarterback. He played 13 seasons with the Vikings. Tarkenton led the team to the Super Bowl three times. He was the NFL **Most Valuable Player (MVP)** in 1975. Carl Eller and Alan Page were two of the toughest Vikings players. They were on the famous "Purple People Eaters" defensive line of the 1960s and 1970s. Page was the NFL MVP in 1971. Defensive linemen Chris Doleman and John Randle were also great. Randle and Doleman played together in the 1990s. Wide receivers Cris Carter and Randy Moss were tough to stop in that era. Both led the NFL in receiving touchdowns three times with the Vikings.

Wide receiver Cris Carter caught his 1,000th career reception in a game against the Detroit Lions on November 30, 2000.

C.CARTER
80
SUPERNAW
29

HEROES NOW

A new star for the Vikings emerged in 2014. It was quarterback Teddy Bridgewater. He started 12 games as a rookie. One of his best targets is tight end Kyle Rudolph. He has battled some injuries. But he shows his skills when he is healthy. Rudolph played all 16 games and made the Pro Bowl in 2012. He was the MVP of the game. The Vikings have strong, young defensive backs, too. Harrison Smith had five interceptions in 2014. Xavier Rhodes is great in coverage.

Quarterback Teddy Bridgewater led the Vikings to three comeback wins in his rookie season.

Vikings
Wilson

GEARING UP

NFL players wear team uniforms. They wear helmets and pads to keep them safe. Cleats help them make quick moves and run fast. Some players wear extra gear for protection.

THE FOOTBALL

NFL footballs are made of leather. Under the leather is a lining that fills with air to give the ball its shape. The leather has bumps or "pebbles." These help players grip the ball. Laces help players control their throws. Footballs are also called "pigskins" because some of the first balls were made from pig bladders. Today they are made of leather from cows.

Tight end Kyle Rudolph runs out for a pass during a game against the New York Giants on October 21, 2013.

HELMET
SHOULDER PADS
GLOVES
THIGH PADS
FOOTBALL
CLEATS

SPORTS STATS

ere are some of the all-time career records for the Minnesota Vikings. All the stats are through the 2014 season.

RECEPTIONS

Cris Carter 1,004

Randy Moss 587

RUSHING YARDS

Adrian Peterson 10,190

Robert Smith 6,818

TOTAL TOUCHDOWNS

Cris Carter 110

Randy Moss 93

INTERCEPTIONS

Paul Krause 53

Bobby Bryant 51

SACKS

John Randle 114

Chris Doleman 96.5

POINTS

Fred Cox 1,365

Cris Carter 670

Quarterback Fran Tarkenton played for Minnesota from 1961 to 1966 and 1972 to 1978.

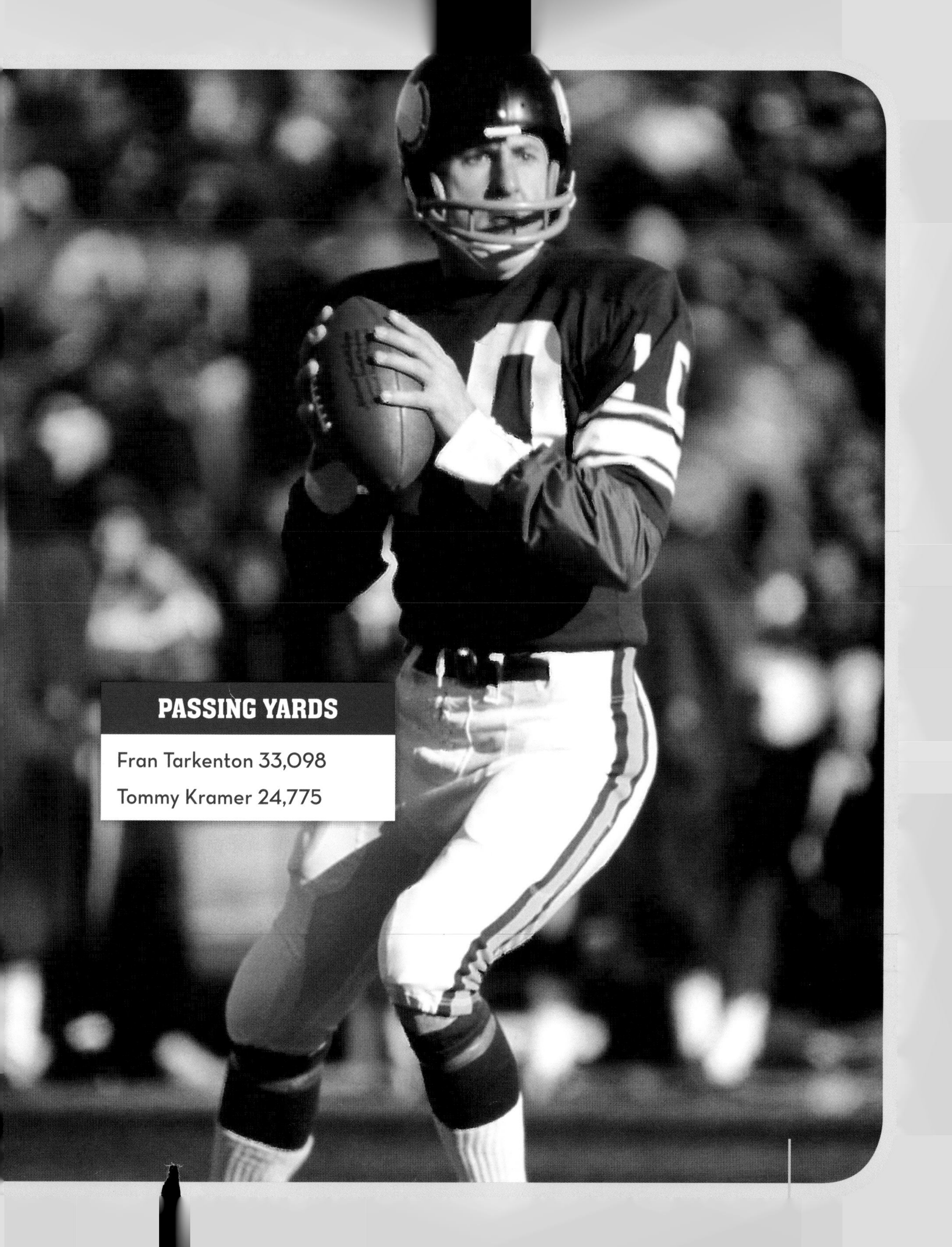
PASSING YARDS
Fran Tarkenton 33,098
Tommy Kramer 24,775

GLOSSARY

citizens people that live in a certain city

league an organization of sports teams that compete against each other

Most Valuable Player (MVP) a yearly award given to the top player in the NFL

playoffs a series of games after the regular season that decides which two teams play in the Super Bowl

rivals teams whose games bring out the greatest emotion between the players and the fans on both sides

rookie a player playing in his first season

Super Bowl the championship game of the NFL, played between the winners of the AFC and the NFC

touchdown a play in which the ball is held in the other team's end zone, resulting in six points

FIND OUT MORE

IN THE LIBRARY

Bruton, Jim. *Vikings 50: All Time Greatest Players in Franchise History*. Chicago: Triumph Books, 2012.

Editors of Sports Illustrated Kids. *Sports Illustrated Kids Football: Then to WOW!* New York: Sports Illustrated, 2014.

Gilbert, Sara. *NFL Today: Minnesota Vikings*. Mankato, MN: Creative Paperbacks, 2013.

ON THE WEB

Visit our Web site for links about the Minnesota Vikings:
childsworld.com/links

Note to Parents, Teachers, and Librarians: We routinely verify our Web links to make sure they are safe and active sites. So encourage your readers to check them out!

INDEX